Malware

By Solis Tech

Malware Detection & Threats Made Easy!

2nd Edition

Table of Contents

Introduction

I want to thank you and congratulate you for purchasing the book, *"Malware: Malware Detection & Threats Made Easy!"*.

This book contains proven steps and strategies on how to avoid, detect and remove malware.

Malware creators are very creative, employing both technical and social means to spread malware. Simply installing antivirus software is no longer enough. This book explains how malware spreads in order to arm the reader with information on how to manage its threat.

Thanks again for purchasing this book, I hope you enjoy it!

Chapter 1 – Malware

Computers are inherently dumb. They can accept and input data, can process it at high-speed, and can return the results almost instantly. However, users need to tell the computer what to do in the form of codes. We call these codes programs, applications, scripts or software, but they are essentially the same. They give instructions to the computer. What the computer does will depend on the instructions given to it. Tell it to do something useful and it will. Give it instructions to perform a malicious task and it will do it without question. Even computers with artificial intelligence are simply following instructions that simulate human's way of thinking.

Computers do not care who gives the instructions. As long as the instructions are loaded into memory, the computer will process it accordingly. Upon startup, a short set of instructions will tell the computer to load and launch the operating system or OS. The OS in turn executes startup instructions that it finds. These include preparing the input and output drivers, as well as launching other background tasks. Having done that, the OS awaits command from its user to execute other applications.

Malware developers take advantage of these key concepts. They find vulnerabilities in the operating and network system that will allow them to install malware and have it running in the background. Vulnerabilities are bugs in the program that can let malware writers load additional code and execute it. These bugs or programming errors do not always appear during the testing stage.

Some malware writers use social engineering to trick victims into installing malware into their computers. They use the computer's connection to internal and external networks to propagate the malware. They infect shared storage to spread malware among colleagues. They hack into servers to install malicious code that will infect site visitors. They can do this because computers will run any executable code that is loaded into its memory.

What is Malware?

Malware is short for malicious software. It is a general term for a code that compromises a computer and instructs it to do malicious tasks, often without the knowledge or permission from the computer's owner. Early malware refers to programming challenges and pranks like programs that delete user files, but recent malware refers to targeting servers to make them inaccessible or for financial gains.

Home computers are not safe, either. Cybercriminals are using home computers to launch attacks on servers in addition to stealing personal information to access online bank accounts. Some advertisers adopt malware, too. They no longer wait for users to visit their sites, but install malware into a victim's computer so they can modify browser settings and change the default home page, eventually advertising their products every time a user opens the browser. They sometimes change the default search engine, replacing it with engines that track user habits to benefit advertisers.

Mobile devices are not safe, either. Today's mobile devices are computers with features and capabilities that are comparable to older computers. Mobile devices, like smartphones and tablets, are vulnerable because they require applications to work. If users inadvertently download a compromised application, then there is a possibility that malware can compromise their mobile devices, too.

A future malware playground is Internet of Things. It is a term for consumer devices like smart home appliances and vehicles loaded with small computers to provide intelligent functionality. These intelligent appliances connect to the Internet for remote control and administration. Having computers on these things, it may not be long until we can see malware on these devices too.

Remember that appliance manufacturers are not IT companies; hence, they may not have the capability to implement data security in their products. A hacker compromising a manufacturer's server could trigger a firmware update on connected appliances and make it perform additional functions, including attacking other servers on the Internet. It may sound like an event from a science-fiction movie, but this reality is possible.

What is the Difference Between a Malware and a Virus?

Many people confuse malware with viruses. A virus is a type of malware, while malware include viruses and other malicious software.

The first malware were viruses, and developers wrote antivirus software to eliminate these malicious programs. Even when viruses evolved to other forms, people still call them viruses and antivirus companies are using the same term even if they are targeting other malware variants.

Viruses are no longer common on their original form. With antivirus vendors constantly updating their algorithms, malware developers have to come up with new variants to avoid detection, often employing social engineering to propagate malware faster by tricking victims to install it along with legitimate software.

If we look at how malware developers remain active over the years, we can surmise that it is a financially rewarding business; therefore, we can expect cybercriminals to continue developing better malware while antivirus companies play catch-up. The only way to combat malware is to understand the threat it presents, how it spreads and propagates, how to detect it, and how to remove.

What are Potentially Unwanted Programs (PUPs)?

People love free software; however, developers need to earn money too. Malware developers see this as an opportunity to spread malware while providing revenue to free-software developers. What they come up with are installers for legitimate software that also install malware during installation. Antivirus companies call these Potentially Unwanted Programs instead of malware since victims give explicit permission to install them. They have no way of knowing if users allow the installation on purpose or unknowingly installs them.

Why would Users Give Permission to Install PUPs?

Most users do not bother reading user agreements that installers display during installation. Instead, they simply click on the default buttons or press enter. Even if users will read the agreements and prompts, some may not understand the message and assume that they are installing software that is necessary for the main program to work. Unfortunately, PUPs are easy to install, but are often frustrating to remove from the system. Most have more than one instance running such that removing a copy will trigger the second copy to re-install it. Many recent PUPs affect users' browsers, which can be very annoying.

How to Detect the Presence of Malware?

Users familiar with their computer will sometimes notice unusual behavior. Some are obvious, like the browser's looks suddenly changing. Other users may lose their files or the file types are changed. Users may even see system errors that were not present before.

Some changes are not visual, like a program accessing the hard disk and making noise even when the computer is idle. Malware accessing an external server can slow down Internet connection. Infected computers can also be unresponsive when hidden processes are running and using up the computer's memory.

Before assuming that malware may be causing the problem, try restarting the computer and leave it for a few minutes without running any program. If the computer is still slow, then there may be an unwanted background program running, but it still needs confirmation.

On Windows, check the hard disk space by opening any folder and clicking Computer on the left. A hard disk with very little space can slow down the computer and malware may not be the cause.

If there is plenty of hard disk space available, run the Task Manager by holding Ctrl+Alt+Del and selecting it from the menu. Click on the Performance tab and observe the real-time graph. Both the CPU and memory usage should be relatively flat if the computer is idle. An active graph could mean that a hidden program is busy. Click the Applications tab to confirm. There should be no application listed if the user did not execute a program. If there is no program listed and the CPU or memory graph is active then there could be a malware running in the background.

To see the process that is using up the memory, click on the Process tab, then click Memory to display the list in descending order. Check its Image name and description. Right-click on a name, then select Properties to get more details. Use a search engine to validate suspicious names.

The Networking tab can also give clues on the presence of malware. There should be no network activity if the computer is idle. If the network is slow and this graph is active, then a hidden program is accessing an external server or computer.

These are just some ways of detecting the possible presence of malware. Without knowing what the malware exactly is; however, it could be difficult to remove it manually.

Most leading antivirus software can detect and remove malware. For home users, there are free versions available that offer basic protection with the option to purchase upgrades for additional features.

A Note on USB flash drives

With the popularity of USB flash drives, spreading malware via USB is easier. Malware can automatically execute when the user opens a USB flash drive. Once in computer memory, inserting another USB drive will infect it. To prevent this, do not view the contents of a USB flash drive after it mounts. Instead, right-click on the drive's name or icon, then select the scan option from the antivirus. This will remove malware in the flash drive before using it.

If there are signs that a USB drive is infected, but the antivirus does not detect it, install another antivirus program. Some antivirus solutions are not good at detecting USB-based malware.

Antivirus solutions can prevent the installation of malware to some extent. However, there are malware that can still get through if the user is not aware of how they propagate. The best way to prevent malware from infecting computers is to understand how each type works.

The succeeding chapters give an insight into the various forms of malware. It also provides information on how they spread so that users can avoid infecting their computers. Prevention is still the best cure against malware. However, avoiding malware is not easy.

Chapter 2 – Virus

Viruses are the earliest forms of malware and they date back to the time before personal computers became popular. A virus is simply a program that can replicate itself on the same computer. Even without malicious intent, creating many copies of a virus code can quickly fill up the memory and slow the computer down. However, an unmodified virus cannot spread to other computers by itself even if the computers are on a network. Getting the virus inside a computer is the challenge for virus creators.

To avoid detection, virus creators modify legitimate programs by inserting malicious codes. When these programs launch, the virus loads into memory and scans the computer for other executable codes to infect. The virus code stays active in memory until the computer shuts down and the cycle starts again if the user runs the infected program.

Boot Sector Virus

Some viruses attack the boot sector of the computer's bootable disks. The boot sector is an area of a disk that a disk drive initially reads and loads into memory. It contains the startup code that will load other components of the operating system. When the boot sector is infected, the virus loads into memory every time the computer starts, ensuring that it is active without waiting for the user to run an infected program. Since the disk operating system can fit in diskettes in the early days of personal computers, starting a clean computer with an infected bootable diskette can also spread the virus to that computer.

The Different Types of Computer Viruses

IT experts have divided viruses into different types, which are:

Simple Viruses

This type of virus is an important part of any hacker's arsenal. Basically, a simple virus (also known as "pathogen virus") attacks binaries stored on the computer's hard disk. Thus, a simple virus can alter or overwrite the functionality of an innocent file.

In general, simple viruses hide within trusted files. This approach helps them to prevent detection and attain continuous execution (i.e. they will run whenever the user accesses the infected file).

Simple viruses infect computers using the following techniques:

- Parasitism – The virus appends, prepends, or inserts malicious codes into an innocent file. This action allows the virus to control the infected file.

- Links – Here, the virus uses a link to reach the target computer's hard disk.

- Overwriting – The simple virus erases a file and replaces it with malicious codes.

- Duplication – Here, the hacker copies a targeted file. Then, they will insert the virus into the duplicate.

- Source Code – Some hackers add active viruses in the source code of a trusted program.

Encrypted Viruses

An encrypted virus can avoid detection easily. Here, an encryption tool converts the malicious code (which is in plaintext) into ciphertext. This allows the virus to avoid being detected by antivirus engines. The principle was to encode the virus and use an automated decryption tool to install the malicious code into the targeted computer/network.

Oligomorphic Viruses

This kind of virus uses various decryptors to avoid detection and infect the target. An oligomorphic virus can alter available decryptors. However, it cannot alter the encrypted source code.

Polymorphic Viruses

A polymorphic virus can generate an unlimited number of decryptors and use various encryption techniques. Since this type of virus can create countless versions of malicious codes, it can hide from antivirus programs quite easily.

Metamorphic Viruses

A metamorphic virus doesn't have a stable body or decryptor. With every generation, the virus alters its body to prevent detection. The code that triggers the alteration is placed inside the virus itself.

Basically, metamorphic viruses don't alter their code completely. They just change their functionality (e.g. using new registers, changing flow controls, rearranging independent commands, etc.). These alterations fool antivirus programs without affecting the malware.

EPO Viruses

EPO (i.e. Entry-Point Obscuring) viruses write codes at random areas inside the infected program. This forces the program to run the virus instead of its own codes. Since the malware operates within a trusted program, the antivirus present in the machine will have a hard time detecting the attack.

Be Careful when Using Shared Resources

Viruses can spread through sharing. When a user mounts a removable storage media on an infected computer while a virus is active, the virus attempts to infect programs that it finds on the mounted media as well. In the early days, this applies to floppy diskettes and external hard drives, but infections are more common today on flash USB drives.

Once the user connects an infected storage to another computer and runs an infected program, the virus activates and infects the other programs in the new computer as well. This makes users who mount USB drives on shared computers at risk if the computer has no sufficient antivirus protection installed. For this reason, avoid connecting USB drives at Internet cafes and on other public computers.

Even shared documents can carry viruses. Some productivity software allows scripts or macros to automate common tasks. Scripts and macros are small, but powerful programs; hence, they can spread viruses, too. Executing an infected macro will also compromise other documents on the same computer. Worse, sending a copy of an infected document can also infect the receiver's computer.

Are Early Viruses Malicious?

Some early viruses started as programming challenges. There was a game that was named Core Wars where the objective is to create a program that loads in memory, then replicate and terminate other programs running on the same memory space. The competing programs create copies of the code while overwriting enemy codes to terminate them. The program that remains in control is the winner.

Other early versions are simply annoying. Two programmers wrote the Brain virus because users were illegally copying their diskettes. The Brain virus simply displays information about the programmers. The Brain virus spread to computers in other countries.

Computers were not widely connected before and the worst thing that a virus can do is to delete files or make them inaccessible. This is exactly what early destructive viruses did. Some programmers wrote viruses that display something interesting while deleting computer files.

Birth of Antivirus Companies

It was not long before other programmers started writing codes to remove viruses, turning the process into a never-ending game of cat and mouse. Virus creators are continually discovering new computer vulnerabilities that they can take advantage of, while antivirus developers update their codes to combat new virus strains. It has become a never ending battle between malware developers and antivirus companies.

Antivirus programs initially identify specific viruses using their signatures. Signatures are like patterns or fingerprints that identify specific viruses. Virus creators responded by continually creating virus variants that require new methods of detection to keep up. This is why antivirus programs update their databases almost daily.

Antivirus can only play catch up if they rely solely on signatures. Modern antivirus programs detect possible viruses by their behavior in addition to signatures.

Most free antivirus software in the market can eliminate common virus threats so not having one installed is not an excuse. While they retain the name, current antivirus software can detect and remove other forms of malware. To enable additional protection, users can purchase additional features.

However, those who do not have a budget for paid features can still protect themselves from malware. The key is to understand how other forms of malware spread. The next chapters will explain these.

Chapter 3 - Worms

While viruses were a threat due to their ability to replicate, it is not a tool for mass infection because it cannot spread to other computers. The capability to spread over the network by itself is a feature of worms. Networks include local area networks (LAN) that are commonly found in offices, Wide Area Network (WAN) for remote offices, as well as worldwide networks like the Internet.

Early worm research had good intentions and started as helpful ideas. One worm crawls networked computers at night to run processor-intensive tasks, but saves the work and stays idle during the day so people can use the computers normally. It is a good idea that maximizes computer resources, similar to how modern cloud computing works. However, a programming error caused the computers to crash and they had to write another program to remove it.

Another programmer wrote a seemingly harmless worm to check the size of the Internet. The worm creates copies on target computers as it moved from one computer to the next. Due to a programming decision, it can install a copy even if it already exists on the same computer. Multiple running copies of the same worm can slow down the computer until it eventually crashes. A single worm was able to crash a big part the Internet.

Worms spread across the network by exploiting operating system and application vulnerabilities and taking advantage of insufficient data security practices. Nowadays, worms can also spread through social engineering. Social engineering is a technique used by hackers to trick users into unknowingly breaking standard data security precautions. Hackers can bypass a highly secure environment using social engineering.

Operating systems, or OS, are programs that manage computers and network equipment. Just like any program, it can have unintentional bugs and updating usually fixes the problem. Worms take advantage of these vulnerabilities to compromise the system.

If the OS or application developer releases an update before someone announces the vulnerability, then users have time to update the operating system before a malware exploits the vulnerability. This is why users should install updates especially if the patch is to address data security issues. Allowing automatic updates usually takes care of this, although there is a risk of automatically installing buggy updates.

On the other hand, if a malware creator releases a worm before the developer discovers the bug and releases an update, what we have is zero-day vulnerability. Modern antivirus companies address this by developing algorithms that detect malicious behavior. However, very aggressive antivirus solutions may lead to false positives.

False positives result when a scan reports the presence of malicious code when there is none. A good antivirus has few false positives. Third party evaluations can determine effective antivirus solutions with fewer false positives.

Mass-mailer worms

Worms can access email clients on user computers and use it to email copies of the worm to contacts in the address book. Some of these emails can trick recipients into downloading and installing the attachment, compromising the receiver's computer in the process. When this happens, that computer also becomes a mass-mailing tool. Unfortunately, these worms can also get a name from the address book and change the From field with this name. This means that the sender in the email may not be the email source, making the source difficult to track.

Aside from possibly compromising recipients' computers, mass mailers can also slow down network performance. If a worm infects several computers on the same network, then it could eat up all the allocated bandwidth. Worse, data security companies may include the computer's IP address in the blacklist for spamming. This can affect all computers in the network that shares the same public IP.

This is because most offices and home networks use a single public IP address for their router while individual computers get private IP addresses. Worse, some DSL subscribers may get a banned public IP address when their router restarts.

Always be wary of unsolicited emails with attachment even if it comes from a trusted source. A possible indicator of spam mail is when the receiver's name is not mentioned in the salutation. Bad grammar is also a sign of possible spam email.

Do not assume that the antivirus can catch all worm variants. Some worms change the file extension of the attached file. Users may think that they are opening an image file when in reality they are executing a worm. Worms do this by adding a .jpg to the filename, like picture.jpg.exe. Since many users configure their computers to hide the file extension, they do not see that the real extension is .exe because the filename they see is picture.jpg.

Some mass-mailer worms simply send spam advertisements. While they may not do damage to a user's computer, they can still trick victims into purchasing illegitimate products. These emails often have a web beacon, a small image that is loaded from an external server. Displaying this image will send the user's email address to the server, thereby validating that it is an active email account. It will then be a target for future spam emails.

Note that spammers do not use their own computers to send mass emails. They use email worms to prevent authorities from easily tracking them.

Worms for Phishing

Mass-mailer worms provide a great platform for quickly distributing malware. Malware creators use these worms to transport different payloads depending on their intention. One application of mass-mailers is for phishing.

Phishing is a form of identity fraud and is usually for stealing personal information for financial gains. It works this way.

Malware creators will copy a legitimate website's looks, specifically the login and profile pages. Websites of financial institutions like banks and payment platforms are examples of these. Next, they will create an email that looks like an official document coming from the target institutions. These emails often have a sense of urgency, requiring the user to log in to the website immediately to validate or change the password for security purposes. It will also include a link to the appropriate page for the user's convenience.

There lies the trick. Instead of linking to the legitimate page, it will redirect the user to the fake login page after clicking the email link. The URL will have the legitimate website's domain name, but with added characters. Some users may mistakenly believe that they are in the genuine site and proceed to log in. After entering the login detail, the next page may even require them to enter their credit card details for validation.

In reality, users can enter anything in the login page and it will be successful. The login page will simply save the credentials entered by the user, then display a page to get other credentials. When in doubt, users can initially enter incorrect login credentials to check if the site can really validate their account. If it accepts a wrong username or password, then there is no validation and the site is a fake.

Another way to verify if a website is a fake is through browsing all the menus and internal links before entering the login details. Malware creators may not go through the trouble of recreating an entire website's content.

To guard against phishing, never click on an email link to log in or change account details. Always type the known URL on the browser address bar. If clicking an email link asks the user to log in, then do not continue. Instead, type the correct URL in the browser's address bar before logging in.

The next chapter discusses other payloads that worms usually bring.

Chapter 4 - Trojan Horse

Trojans are malware that disguise as useful programs or install together with a legitimate application. Its name comes from the Trojan War, a part of Greek mythology where a wooden gift horse had soldiers inside that attacked the enemies while they were asleep to win the war. Similarly, a Trojan pretends to be a useful application, waiting for the user to launch it to execute the malicious code. Once activated, trojans will run in the background to do their designated task.

Trojans do not replicate and spread by themselves. They often combine with worms to infect other computers. Trojans are also common on unsolicited email attachments, while some users download them along with valid applications.

There are several types of trojans according to function.

Root kits

Root kit is not inherently bad. It is originally a tool for system administrators. It becomes bad if the creator installs it on a computer without permission from the owner, especially if the purpose is to do malicious tasks.

Some trojans will modify the computer's system for hackers to gain access. Root kits are tools for administrators that hide in the operating system while providing a back door for their creator. With privileged access, a root kit's owner can do almost anything to the infected computer remotely. Root kits are good at hiding their existence, making them difficult to detect. They can also delete any traces of malware installation. Root kits usually remain hidden until activated.

Since rootkits play an important part in today's hacking attacks, a whole chapter is dedicated to them. You'll learn more about this kind of malware later.

Bots

Bots are programs that perform automated tasks. Some bots, called spambots, flood websites with spam advertisements to generate traffic for another website. This is common in online forums and is the main reason why websites validate users before accepting their registration details. Some registration forms require the user to type the characters shown on an image to validate that the applicant is human. However, some spammers go around this by hiring humans to solve the test, although it comes at a cost.

A more malicious bot is one that employs brute-force attack on target websites. Most website owners do not build websites from scratch, but simply use an open source Content Management System (CMS) as a starting point. A CMS is a fully functioning website that allows the user to update content without writing a single line of HTML code. There are many templates to choose from, and websites owners can customize further by using their own graphic images. Using CMS, owners can update website content in a few clicks.

Many CMS software have the default username "admin" and some website owners do not bother changing it. Given the default administrator name, hackers only need to guess the password to take over the website and install malicious software. If it is a popular forum, then there is a risk that hackers can steal the member database.

To attack a website, hackers write bots that log into the target website and try to log in with passwords taken from a table of common passwords as well as words from the dictionary. A website that does not limit failed logins in a given period is a good target. Using a network of zombie computers, hackers are able to brute-force attack a website using bots with minimal risk of authorities tracking the attack's mastermind.

Stolen password databases from forums are not safe, either. Using rainbow tables, hackers can use brute-force to find the matching password for a member account. Since many users employ the same username and password on all sites they register to, this allows the hackers to hack into members' accounts on other sites as well.

Remote-controlled Bots

Malware developers can turn an infected computer into a remote-controlled bot that will perform malicious tasks, including attacking another computer. This is how they get away with Distributed Denial of Service attacks. Attackers do not use their own computers to flood a server, but instead, they use a large network of zombie computers from unsuspecting users. This also saves the attacker from bandwidth costs since the computer owner is paying for it. It also makes it difficult to track the attacker after it spreads from one computer to another.

One analysis of an affected computer shows that bots log into a chat server, waiting for commands from its master. Think of an army of sleeper bots just waiting patiently for a command to attack. Developers will typically just let an installed Trojan do nothing until they have an army of remote-controlled bots to launch a large-scale cyber-attack. The attacker then issues the command to attack from the chat server where the bots log in each time the infected computer is running.

Without good anti-malware software, the presence of a remote-controlled bot in a computer is difficult to detect since it sleeps until a command is given.

Keylogger

Some trojans can capture keystrokes as well as mouse movements in the background without the user knowing it. Called keyloggers, these programs can serve as surveillance software for a good purpose. Some parents use it to monitor children's online activity.

17

Trojan keyloggers can steal passwords and other personal credentials from unsuspecting users. It can wait for specific events, like users opening a login page, before starting to record user actions and keystrokes. It then sends the log to a remote server for its master.

Spyware

Spyware is another Trojan that collects sensitive information similar to a keylogger. However, it is not limited to monitoring key strokes to steal user credentials, but can also gather information about the user's online activity as well.

Basically, a spyware program compiles data about a person or a group of people without their knowledge. This kind of program usually steals data that can be used for financial gain or advertising purposes.

A spyware can steal different types of information: login credentials, DNS and Internet Protocol addresses, browsing habits, or even financial data (e.g. bank details, credit/debit card information, etc.). Among all spyware programs that hackers use, the most dangerous ones are those that capture information related to banking. IT experts refer to these programs as "banker Trojans."

Trj/Sinowal, a spyware kit sold on Russian websites, is a great example for this category. Hackers used this program to launch attacks against websites that offer online banking.

Who Sends Spyware Programs?

These computer programs are written by cyber-criminals, who offer them to thieves and fraudsters.

Many people are confused with what spyware programs really are. This confusion exists because some individuals consider some toolbars and adware programs as spyware. The main difference between adware and spyware is that adware programs are used by online marketers while spyware programs are used by criminals.

How Does a Spyware Program Reach Its Victim?

Hackers install spyware programs without the victim's knowledge or consent. They perform the installation process while the victim downloads a file, installs another program, or visits an infected site.

In general, spyware programs infect a computer when the user installs a different application. Hackers offer free programs that attract potential victims. These victims don't know that the programs they're getting are rigged with spyware.

How Can You Prevent Spyware Attacks?

You can protect yourself from spyware programs by following these tips:

- Be careful when downloading materials through P2P (i.e. Peer-to-Peer) networks.

- Don't download any material from unknown or suspicious sites.

- Make sure that your computer has an antivirus program.

- If an unknown program has infected your machine, try to remove it through the Control Panel.

Adware

Adware is similar to spyware, but simply records and sends users' online activity and behavior as marketing data to marketers so they can display an appropriate advertisement. Some versions will redirect browser searches to advertisements while others will replace the default search engine with an advertiser's search engine.

Adware creators write these malware for revenue generation. Adware that alters browser settings is very difficult to remove. Antivirus software can remove adware from the computer, but usually leaves the modified browser settings. Saving browser bookmarks and restoring to factory settings can sometimes fix the problem.

Ransomware

Ransomware does what its name suggests. After installing the malicious code, it will either prevent access to the infected computer or encrypt the contents of its hard disk. Users will see a message demanding payment to disable the malware. The criminals behind typically employ money transfer services that are difficult to track. Add this to the fact that these cybercriminals usually live in other countries, making it difficult to run after them.

To spread ransomware, cybercriminals typically take over a legitimate website, usually without the owner's knowledge, to install the malware. They can also spread ransomware using drive-by downloads on the compromised website.

Drive-by Download

A drive-by download will allow the installation of malware by simply browsing an infected website. The user does not even have to click a download link. The affected website contains codes that check for browser or operating system vulnerabilities that allow for automatic download. The malware will install a program with a task to connect to another server to download the rest of the malware. The victim may not notice the download due to the initial programs' small size.

Some anti-malware software can warn if a website has malware when a user tries to access it.

Suspicious Packers

In order to avoid detection, suspicious packers compress and encrypt malware code. Good anti-malware utilities are aware of this and are able to detect the behavior of suspicious packers and prevent them from executing.

Removing Trojans

Most antivirus companies have software that can automatically remove trojans. While it is possible to remove Trojans manually, this may be a challenge since many have multiple copies running that can reinstall copies if the user deletes one.

When looking for good antivirus software, try the demo versions first. If satisfied, users can pay for other features that provide complete protection to the computer. Some of these protections include email and web surfing security.

In some cases, antivirus software can remove malware from the system, but not from the browser. If removing browser add-ons and restoring to factory setting does not work, uninstall the browser and download again.

Avoiding Installer Trojans

Among the popular sources of Trojans are free software installers. Software development costs money, and offering it free is not good for business. However, many people would prefer free over paid versions, especially when performing simple or one-time tasks. To address this, developers break down their programs by specific features, then allow third party marketers to offer them as free downloads in return for revenue to the developer. For example, one utility can convert AVI formats to MP4, while another can convert MP4 to MPG.

How can marketers earn money from offering free downloads? They get revenue by offering their services to advertisers. These marketers create installers for legitimate software, then include the option to install software from other companies. There is nothing wrong with that right, except that many users do not bother reading what they are installing. Unfortunately, many of these optional programs are adware that antivirus software tag as Potential Unwanted Programs (PUP).

An installer for free software will first confirm that users want to install the desired legitimate program. After the user clicks on the Continue or Next button, the installer will get the user's consent to install additional software along with a few descriptions of its benefits. Sometimes, the installer will display an End User License Agreement (EULA), something that no one ever reads, but simply agrees to. It is common to see more than one program added in the installation. The problem, however, is that the default buttons will install these extra programs if the user is not careful.

How can users avoid these additional installations, especially if the user is unsure if the other software is required? Most installers have a Decline button for optional installations. When an installer shows the Decline button, then that additional software is probably a PUP. Pay attention to the presence of Decline buttons.

Some installers have no separate dialog boxes for additional software installation. Instead, easy and custom install options are available, with the easy install as the default. What the user may not see is that the easy install option will sometimes install additional software. Click the custom install option when it is available and deselect unfamiliar applications.

Some antivirus may give an alert that the installer has a Trojan. Always scan the installer after downloading. Users can do this by selecting the installer, right clicking then selecting the Scan option to run the antivirus. This is also a good practice after inserting USB devices.

Users can perform additional verification after each installation. In Windows, simply select Programs and Features from the control panel, then click the Installed On tab. Sort the list in descending order. The programs with the current date are the ones included in the installation. Select suspicious programs and click uninstall. To verify applications, enter the program name in a search engine to see what it does.

Chapter 5 – Threats on Mobile Devices

Mobile technology is now a part of people's everyday lives. Smartphones today are very powerful. They are no longer just for voice and text, but for accessing the Internet and playing games as well. Though not as efficient as personal computers, users can perform most tasks on their smartphones.

For those who require laptop capability at more portable form factor, tablets are a blessing. Those who want the small size of a phone, but with a bigger screen like a tablet, can choose a phablet. Mobile computing is now a reality.

As computers, these mobile devices can be targets of malware. To minimize these, Android and IOS, the leading mobile platforms, have screening policies in place to reduce the chances of malware getting into the official stores. Additionally, updates to the operating system often include security fixes for known vulnerabilities to strengthen the security of devices. Installing the latest updates, when available to the user's mobile device, addresses possible malware problems.

By default, users can only download apps from the official stores. This is Google Play for Android and App Store for IOS. However, a checkbox on Android's setting will allow the user to download from any external server. There lies the problem.

The price for mobile apps is quite low compared to their PC counterparts. However, many users still do not wish to pay for the apps they download, despite their low prices. Malware creators take advantage of this by making commercial apps available for free download on third party servers. By simply deselecting a default Android setting, users can now download a paid app for free.

Unfortunately, for them, these modified apps may contain malware written for mobile devices. Once installed on a mobile device and executed, these malware take over the device and do what PC malware often do. Some malware may steal user credentials while others may display unwanted advertisements. These malware can make the devices very slow, rendering them unusable. Restoring to factory settings may be the only option for some.

IOS has no checkbox to allow downloading of apps from unofficial sites, but bugs in the operating systems can allow jailbreaks. Jailbreaks are IOS hacks that allow users to customize their devices. It also allows users to install unofficial apps. Some of these apps may have malware and can compromise the device.

Malware creators are smart and can always find ways around a secure system. One company created a Windows application that allows users to download apps for free then transfer them to their IOS device. This comes with a risk, however, since some of these apps may also have malware.

Malware creators started targeting IOS developers in China. They did this by making local copies of Apple's development platform since downloading from Apple's official servers is quite slow for developers located in China. Unfortunately, the unofficial installer has malware that infects the apps they are developing. Some of these apps made their way into the App Store before they were discovered and removed.

Another malware creator took advantage of enterprise certificates. These certificates are used by companies to install their own apps on IOS devices without approval from Apple. Malware creators are tricking users to install an enterprise certificate so they can install apps with malware on victims' devices. Many users who do not understand the implications are at risk.

Apple quickly released an update to IOS that prevents this malware from installing. Those who are still using an older version of IOS can also avoid this malware by not allowing the installation of certificates unless it is from their company's IT department.

For IOS users, downloading apps only from the App Store can minimize the risk of malware. It does not mean that Android users are safer, though. Malware writers are invading Google Play by creating fake apps that mimic original apps, but with additional malware. Google has to monitor millions of apps and ensuring that apps do not have malware is not easy. There is a way to avoid potential malware, though. If an Android app asks for unnecessary permissions during installation, do not install it.

Fortunately, antivirus companies now have versions for both the IOS and Android platforms. Installing these apps will help users screen potential malware during installation, as well as remove malware that were accidentally installed.

Chapter 6: How Computer Systems Get Infected

The IT landscape is more dangerous than ever before. The technological advancements you are enjoying right now are empowering computer hackers – people who want to access your network and utilize it for their bad intentions. These people might target you using emails or websites and ask you to provide confidential pieces of information (e.g. usernames, passwords, credit card number, etc.). Nowadays, hackers fool their victims by creating credible-looking websites and emails. That means you can't rely on your eyes or intuition in checking whether you are electronically safe or not.

This chapter will discuss the main techniques that hackers use to infect and access computer systems. It will expound the lessons you've learned in the earlier chapters by providing real-world and theoretical examples.

The Techniques Used by Hackers in Propagating Malware

Traditionally, malware attacks focus on applications (e.g. Notepad, Microsoft Word, Microsoft Excel, etc.) and platforms (e.g. Linux, Microsoft Windows, Mac OS, etc.). Some malicious pieces of software were actually distributed by program manufacturers and included directly in the installation discs of their products. Two of the most popular malware propagation techniques used in the 90s were "email attacks" and direct program execution. However, these attacks are no longer effective (thanks to the improvements in malware detection products and programs).

In this section of the book, you'll learn about the standard techniques used by hackers in spreading their malware. Study this material carefully since it will arm you with useful information regarding computer security.

Social Engineering

This technique, which involves the violation of a person's trust, is perhaps the oldest form of malware propagation in the whole world. Despite its age, it is still one of the most effective techniques that hackers have in their arsenal.

Basically, this technique involves the creation of a story that is shared with a victim. The attacker hopes that the victim will believe the story and perform the required steps to install and activate the malware. Often, the victim doesn't know about the actual attack, although the story or delivery used by the hacker is shallow. In some cases, the victim feels that something is wrong and discovers the hacker's plot after a fast introspection. The security team of the company/organization then tries to eliminate the malicious software and stop its propagation inside the computer network.

According to some security experts, no malware can infect a computer system without using this technique. The following screenshots show real-world examples of social engineering attacks. As you can see, these images try to build a false sense of security. Careless users will surely click on them or even provide confidential information.

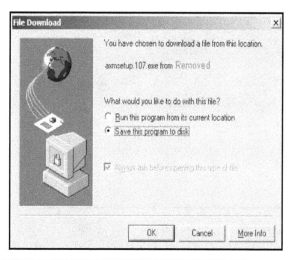

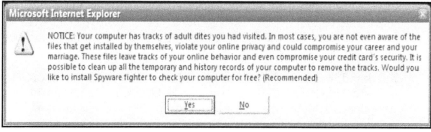

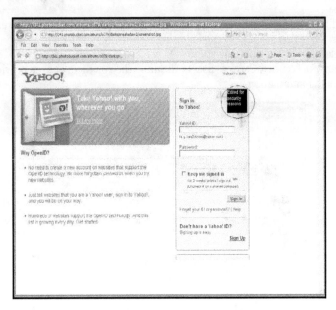

File Execution

Security experts consider this as the simplest technique for malware propagation. The malware installs itself onto the computer system once the victim clicks on the infected file. Generally, hackers who use this technique rename the dangerous file or embed it into a different file. These tactics help them in disguising the malware and fooling their victims.

Attackers deliver the infected file using social engineering (which was discussed earlier) or technical methods (e.g. email attacks, file sharing, P2P or peer-to-peer networking, etc.). These days, some hackers deliver their malware through downloadable computer games. That means you have to be careful when downloading files onto your computer. The last thing you want to happen is to compromise your computer's security just because of a boring game.

Some infected files appear as plain graphic animations, spreadsheet tables, presentation slides, or even horror stories. Many people think of "file execution" as the basis of other malware propagation techniques. Basically, if you won't execute the affected file, the malware won't infect your computer/network. The table below shows you some of the file types that hackers use in delivering malware to their victims.

File Extension	Required Computer Program
.doc	Microsoft Word
.pdf	Adobe Reader

.ppt	Microsoft PowerPoint
.exe	None
.flv	Flash Player
.bat	None
.xls	Microsoft Excel

The old types of malware were created to destroy the affected machine/computer. Several decades ago, attackers simply wanted to show their creativity by releasing destructive codes and programs. That's the reason why they used simple and detectable propagation methods. These hackers lost their effectiveness when software manufacturers released antivirus programs in the market.

The Modern Propagation Techniques

IDSs (i.e. Intrusion Detection Systems) are now having problems detecting malware propagation techniques. These problems result from the recent advancements in network services, system applications, and OS (i.e. operating system) features. Some IDSs are practically useless against new types of malware. At the start of the 21st century, hackers started to use new techniques in spreading their malicious programs.

The list below shows some of the most popular malware in history.

- StormWorm – This malware was released back in 2007. It infected computers through file execution and email attacks. To spread this malware, hackers used the following techniques:

  o File Deletion/Overwrite

  o Fast Flux Chaining

  o P2P Structure Attacks

- AutoIT – This malware became popular back in 2008. It infected computers through file execution. Hackers generated countless copies of AutoIT into removable file storages by overwriting "autorun.inf".

- Downdup – Hackers released this malware back in 2009. They used file execution to inject it into the computers of their victims. These hackers targeted users or networks with weak passwords. Once access had been secured, the "bad guys" propagated the malware inside the network by sharing and transferring the infected file.

27

- Bacteraloh – Hackers launched this malware on P2P networks. They disguised it as a utility file that can be downloaded and executed locally.

- Koobface – Attackers used this malware on the client-side of their targeted networks. Basically, these attackers propagated the Koobface malware using social networking sites (e.g. Friendster, MySpace, Facebook, etc.). They used URLS that were linked to the said malware.

StormWorm – The Most Elusive Computer Worm in History

Stormworm is a worm that sends spam emails. According to computer experts, StormWorm used social engineering to find targets. It employed Microsoft Office-related files (e.g. spreadsheets, slides, documents, etc.) that are loaded with malicious codes to get the email information of its victims.

Basically, StormWorm is a Trojan horse that relies on backdoor and P2P botnet framework for propagation and installation. Also, it used Microsoft operating systems to infect computers. StormWorm utilizes the P2P botnet framework (a new control and command technique) to improve its persistence and survivability.

In a P2P botnet, no one computer has a complete list of the network. Each computer has limited information about the network it belongs to. Also, these machines are interconnected – they are spread out like a complicated net, making it extremely hard to measure the real scope of the affected network. Computer experts failed to calculate the size of this worm. However, these experts claim that StormWorm created the biggest botnet in history, with about 10 million affected networks.

Once a system has been infected, this worm will install a file named Win32.Agent.dh, which resulted in the destruction of the earlier versions created by the author/s. Many IT professionals thought that this flow can be a weapons test of a large organization since the original host code contained flaws that can be easily stopped.

The Methods Hackers Use in Hiding Malware

Hackers use different methods in hiding their malicious programs. In this section, you'll learn about these methods in detail. Study this material carefully since it contains useful information regarding malware detection.

Metamorphism

Metamorphic malwares change as they propagate or reproduce, making them hard to detect through signature-based antivirus programs. The difference between each variant is minimal – it's just enough to allow the variant to infect other computer systems. This method depends highly on the algorithm employed to trigger the mutations. If the hacker/s didn't implement this method properly, you may use certain countermeasures to anticipate the iterations of the malware. The diagram below shows how every mutation of the malware is altered just enough to prevent the antivirus program from detecting the attack.

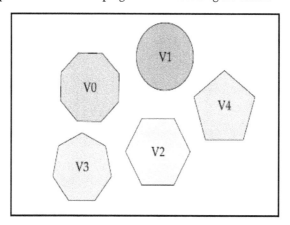

Hackers have been using this method for many years. The techniques in which malwares mutate inside a machine have improved greatly. Thus, detecting and stopping malware infections have become extremely difficult.

Polymorphism

The term "polymorphism" refers to self-reproducing malwares that assume different structures than the first one. It is a type of camouflage that was used by malware authors to bypass the string searches conducted by modern antivirus programs. Basically, the encryption and mutation processes employed in polymorphism have evolved continuously. That means the developments attained by antivirus companies are completely useless.

The following image shows the common mutation process used by polymorphic malwares:

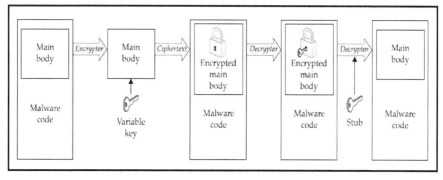

Oligomorphism

29

IT experts consider this technique as the "poor man's" version of polymorphism. Oligomorphic malwares choose a decryptor from a predetermined set of alternatives. Basically, you can identify/detect these predetermined alternatives using a set of decryptors. The diagram below will help you understand this technique further:

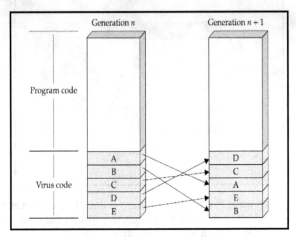

Obfuscation

Modern hackers obfuscate their malware in different ways. The most popular type of obfuscation is packing the malware's source code through encryption or compression (which will be discussed later). According to IT security experts, code obfuscation is one of the important topics related to malicious programs and hacking attacks. Often, hackers use network and host obfuscation to bypass both kinds of security measures.

In some cases, obfuscation can result to the downfall of a malware. For example, network defenders may use the obfuscation techniques implemented by the attacker to generate signatures for malware detection. In the next pages, you'll learn about important facts related to malware obfuscation.

The Oldest Forms of Obfuscation

The following list shows you the obfuscation techniques used by hackers in infecting computer systems.

- "Archivers" – Before, hackers used CAB, TAR, RAR, and ZIP utilities to obfuscate malicious programs. For an archiver to work, it must be installed on the targeted host unless the creator has provided the utility in the loader. Attackers no longer use this method since the malware must unpack and move to the hard disk before it can execute. Thus, the victim's antivirus software can easily detect and stop the malware propagation.

30

- Encryptors – Software developers (i.e. the legit ones) use this technique to protect the source code of their products. They encrypt and compress the source code, making it extremely difficult to reverse engineer.

- Packers – Modern malware programs utilize packers to bypass security measures such as anti-spyware and antivirus programs. Basically, packers are encryption modules that obfuscate the malware's main code (i.e. the code that dictates the malware's functionality). Hackers generally use a packer to get around network-detection tools in transfer and host-based security programs. The private and "single-use" packers are extremely elusive, mainly because they are not available publicly and cannot be identified by commercial security programs.

  In this method, the malicious program doesn't need to reach the hard disk. Everything runs as in-process memory – an approach that can easily bypass security tools.

Modern Obfuscation Techniques

Nowadays, hackers bypass security systems through network encoding. Since most networks allow HTTP/HTTPS to get past security gateways, an encoded malware can infiltrate protection systems without getting detected. Here are some of the most popular variants of network encoding:

- XOR – This is a basic encryption procedure implemented with system communications to prevent detection. Usually, an XOR stream can be found in a security protocol such as SSL (i.e. Secure Socket Layer). Thus, if a security analyst conducts a simple scan, the data traffic would appear encrypted. A deeper analysis, however, would show that the traffic is not SSL.

  XOR is a basic binary operation that takes two binary inputs and gives 0 if the inputs are identical. If the inputs are different, XOR will give 1.

- DDNS (i.e. Dynamic Domain Name Services) – IT experts consider this as the most creative obfuscation technique. At first, this method was used by system administrators to quickly add machines to their network. DDNS gained extreme popularity when Microsoft used it for a program called Active Directory Enterprise System.

  These days, however, hackers use DDNS to access and manipulate systems anonymously. Basically, DDNS is a system where the domain-to-IP resolution can be updated quickly and easily.

- Fast Flux – According to many people, Fast Flux is the most popular obfuscation method for malware. It allows hackers to send content and instructions through a dynamic network of infected hosts. A P2P network environment may also use Fast Flux as a control framework transmitted throughout various servers. When used this way, Fast Flux can be implemented without being detected.

  This method has some similarities with DDNS. However, Fast Flux is better than DDNS in terms of speed and survivability. StormWorm, a malware discussed earlier, used Fast Flux to attack countless systems.

Chapter 7: Rootkits

You've learned about this kind of malware in an earlier chapter. However, since modern hackers consider rootkits as their main weapon, you should arm yourself with more information about this type of software.

Rootkits have evolved over the years. The effectiveness of these malwares has attracted countless hackers worldwide. Thus, you have to be knowledgeable about the features, capabilities, and characteristics of rootkits if you want to protect yourself from the bad guys.

The Main Features of a Rootkit

Maintaining Access

Retaining access to an attacked computer/network is extremely important for a hacker. If he/she can maintain administrative access to a compromised server, the hacker can utilize the network to launch other attacks, store/steal information, or host a website. A rootkit maintains access by installing a local or remote backdoor onto a system. Local backdoors are applications that, once activated, will provide ordinary users with admin privileges.

Because some hackers are actually ordinary users who want to improve their network access, local backdoors serve as an important tool in rootkit development. Additionally, hackers ensure that a local backdoor is available, in case other forms of access (e.g. remote backdoors) stop working.

Remote backdoors provide hackers with excellent benefits. They offer stealth and sophistication – two qualities needed by any hacker. Computer experts divide remote backdoors into three subtypes: Trojan, covert channels, and NSL (i.e. Network Socket Listener).

Stealth

The second main feature of a rootkit is its ability to hide any evidence of its existence. As you probably know, rootkits evolved from computer programs that remove log files from an attacked system. As rootkits began to evolve into programs that provide permanent admin access to the affected host, hackers needed to hide the files and/or registry keys used by their rootkits.

If the malware hides the log files or registry keys used in its operations, the IT personnel and antivirus programs won't detect the attack easily. In general, rootkits hide the following:

- The files they used or generated

- The files specified by the hacker

- The network connections they used or created

The things to be concealed are often written on a configuration file or programmed in the malware itself.

Modern rootkits utilize their stealth capabilities to assist other malicious programs. By combining rootkits and other malware, hackers were able to boost the effectiveness of their attacks.

Different Types of Rootkits

IT experts divide rootkits into two types: (1) user-mode and (2) kernel-mode. A user-mode rootkit runs within a user's context of environment and protection. For instance, if a person accessed his own workstation as a normal user, the malware will provide backdoor access to the computer applications that can be run in that kind of account.

In general, most users have admin privileges. That means user-mode rootkits may also stop network-level processes (e.g. Windows services) from being influenced by its stealth capability.

Kernel-mode rootkits, on the other hand, operate inside the network as an ordinary driver for hardware (e.g. mouse, network card, graphics card, etc.). Creating a kernel-mode rootkit is more complicated than creating a user-mode rootkit. Kernel-mode rootkits also require advanced skills from the hacker in order to conduct attacks successfully. Additionally, since operating systems alter some parts of their kernel with each update and version, kernel-mode rootkits won't work for all versions of an operating system.

Let's discuss each type of rootkit in detail:

User-mode Rootkits

Computer experts define this kind of rootkit as an undetectable collection of code and programs located in "userland" that allows continuous access to a computer or network. The term "userland" refers to the network space that is separated from the kernel. Basically, all user-mode programs run at the "normal user's" level inside the network and not as part of the computer's OS.

For instance, if you accessed your workstation as an ordinary user, the user-mode rootkit will run using your access privileges. All policies and permissions applied to your account will also affect the rootkit that uses your information.

It is true that ordinary users have minimal access to files and directories. However, most users have admin privileges on their respective workstations. Because of that, user-mode rootkits can control an entire workstation.

34

Important Note: The user-mode rootkits included in this chapter are all based on Windows computers. Before we discuss this kind of malware, however, let's review some programming and computing principles related to Windows operating systems. This review will help you to understand the discussion about user-mode rootkits.

Basic Programming and Computing Concepts

- Process – This is an instance of a program being run inside a computer.

- Thread – This is a "subprocess" that performs individual activities. For instance, a single process can generate multiple threads. The distinction between threads and processes is important since most rootkits deal with threads.

- Architecture Rings – In X86 system architecture, protection rings are used to prevent system issues and hacking attacks. These rings offer certain access levels, typically via processor modes.

- System Calls – A user-mode program interacts with the kernel by performing "system calls" (i.e. certain functions taken from the system's dynamic link libraries). When a program makes a system call, the information about the chosen system call is sent to the kernel though a series of function calls. For example, when system call "1" is executed, the system will execute function calls A, B, and C in that particular order.

- Dynamic Link Libraries – These are the libraries shared inside Microsoft operating systems. All DLLs are in PE (i.e. Portable Executable) format, which means they are similar to .exe files. When an application is executed, these libraries load into the system and stay in their location.

- API Functions – Windows computers use APIs (i.e. Application Programming Interfaces) to communicate with any programming language (e.g. C, C++, Java, etc.). If you want more information regarding API elements, you may visit this site: msdn.microsoft.com.

Injection Methods

This section focuses on the complicated functions and methods employed by user-mode rootkits. The initial step for a user-mode rootkit is to install (or inject) its codes into the process it wants to attack. In this part of the book, you'll learn about the modern injection techniques being used by hackers today.

Before rootkits can influence a function and manipulate its execution path, they must inject themselves into the process they want to control. This often involves the installation of a DLL that triggers the execution of the malware's code. If the hacker can't execute the code within the process, the malware won't be able to do anything in the infected computer.

How does "DLL Injection" work? Hackers use three different methods to inject malicious codes into a computer process: (1) Windows Hooks, (2) a variant of CreateRemoteThread, and (3) CreateRemoteThread with LoadLibrary(). Let's discuss each method in detail:

Windows Hooking

Inside a Windows OS, most of the communication for programs that have GUIs (i.e. graphical user interfaces) occur through system messages. Applications that are designed to accept messages will generate a message group that can be used in reading messages from the system. For instance, inside a Windows program, if you'll click on a link using the left-button of your mouse, the system will send a message to the program's message group. Then, the program will read the message, perform the required actions, and wait for the next message.

The image below shows a programming code. It is named Hook.dll, a DLL file designed to export a function call (i.e. HookProcFunc). The HookProcFunc function manages all intercepted messages inside the Windows machine. Inside the hooking installation program, you'll enter the following:

```
bool InstallHook()
{
    HookProc HookProcFunc;
    if (HookProcFunc = (HookProc) ::GetProcAddress (g_hHookDll,"HookProc"))
    {
        if (g_hHook = SetWindowsHookEx(WH_CBT, HookProcFunc, g_hHookDll, 0))
            return true;
    }

    return false;
}
```

As you can see, the code didn't include any statement for loading the DLL. Since HookProc has been injected, the OS will inject the .dll file into all of the processes run by the user and make sure that each message will go to HookProcFunc() before the actual applications (e.g. Internet Explorer) get it. Additionally, HookProcFunc is a simple function. Here's the code that you need to use:

```
LRESULT CALLBACK HookProcFunc(UINT message, WPARAM wParam, LPARAM lParam)
{
      if (message == HCBT_KEYSKIPPED && (lParam & 0x40000000)) {
        if ((wParam==VK_SPACE)||(wParam==VK_RETURN)||
            (wParam==VK_TAB)||(wParam>=0x2f ) &&(wParam<=0x100))   {
            if (wParam==VK_RETURN || wParam==VK_TAB) {
                  WriteKeyStroke('\n');
            } else {
                  BYTE keyStateArr[256];
                  WORD word;
                  UINT scanCode = lParam;
                  char ch;
                  GetKeyboardState(keyStateArr);
                  ToAscii(wParam, scanCode, keyStateArr, &word, 0);
                  ch = (char) word;

                  if ((GetKeyState(VK_SHIFT) & 0x8000) &&
                      wParam >= 'a' && wParam = 'z')
                      ch += 'A'-'a';

                  WriteKeyStroke(ch);
            }
        }
    }
    return CallNextHookEx( 0, message, wParam, lParam);
}
```

This function checks for messages sent by HCBT_KEYSKIPPED. Basically, HCBT_KEYSKIPPED sends a message to HookProcFunc each time the user presses a key on his/her keyboard. The function makes sure that the key presses are valid and maps the characters to each part of the keyboard. If the user presses Enter, the HookProcFunc function will enter a newline character into the log file.

Despite the simplicity of this example, it shows what a hacker needs to do to create a Windows keylogger. With this method, you may also get screenshots of the computer each time a certain Windows message is sent. Some malicious programs are known for capturing images of the entire screen, not just the affected applications.

CreateRemoteThread w/ LoadLibrary()

Hackers use two methods of installing DLL files into various Windows-based processes. The first method involves the function known as CreateRemoteThread. This function begins new threads in the targeted processes. Once a process loads one of these threads, the DLL file will launch a code written by the hacker. This method is easy and simple – hackers have been using this for years.

The argument of CreateRemoteThread() holds the identifier that will be injected by the DLL file. In the current example, the argument is evil_rootkit.dll. To complete the procedure, the malware runs LoadLibrary() (i.e. through GetProcAddress()) once the thread starts in the targeted process.

CreateRemoteThread w/ WriteProcessMemory()

This is the second method used by hackers in injecting DLL files. Rather than forcing the OS to invoke LoadLibrary(), CreateRemoteThread() may run the malware's code. You just have to use WriteProcessMemory() to enter the whole group of functions into the memory space of the process. Then, you'll simply invoke those functions using CreateRemoteThread().

This approach involves several problems. First, it involves multiple processes and data transfers. Second, the hacker also needs to copy different pieces of information (e.g. options, parameters, etc.) manually to complete the process. This is because the codes involved in this technique cannot copy data onto the targeted process.

How to Inject DLL files onto Non-System Processes

In some cases, hackers need to attack processes that are not based on any system. The procedure they use is similar to the approaches discussed above, with one major difference: rather than starting a new thread in the targeted process, the hackers hijack an existing thread and force it to run the malicious code. Once this is accomplished, the hackers release their hold on the abused thread, allowing it to do what it was supposed to do.

Here's how it works:

1. The hackers observe the generation of new processes.

2. Once a new process starts, the hackers look for the first thread's handle.

3. Then, they will invoke SuspendThread() (i.e. a function found in the thread's handle) to stop the thread's execution.

4. The hackers will alter some assembly instructions inside the thread. This way, they can run malicious codes and load the .dll file into the memory space of the targeted process.

According to computer experts, the last step poses the most difficulties for hackers. That's because the hackers should know how processes run and how each register inside the computer's processor works.

Kernel-mode Rootkits

For many experts, kernel-mode rootkits are the oldest and most popular rootkits in the whole world. Additionally, these rootkits pose the most dangerous threats to networks and individual computers. StormWorm, a malware that affected countless machines across several countries almost 10 years ago, possessed a kernel-mode rootkit element. This element allowed StormWorm to infect and damage computers at a deep level – the machine's OS.

Because of this, you have to study this kind of rootkit carefully. You will surely encounter this kind of malware while managing/protecting your own computer or network. The term "kernel-mode" means running on the same level as an OS. Thus, kernel-mode rootkits should know how to utilize the techniques, functions, and structures that actual operating systems use. Also, these rootkits should coexist with the machine's OS while conducting the attack.

This section will discuss the ideas and principles related to operating systems before explaining more facts regarding kernel-mode rootkits. This teaching structure aims to help you understand kernel-mode rootkits completely.

Computer Concepts Related to Kernel Drivers

- The Architecture of Kernel-Mode Drivers – These days, Windows drivers may run in kernel- or user-mode. Kernel-mode drivers communicate with the machine's operating system to manage I/O (i.e. Input/Output) and control the associated device (e.g. mouse, keyboard, graphics card, etc.).

  Each Windows driver should match a driver model and provide normal driver routines. Certain drivers also execute WDM (i.e. Windows Driver Model), which is a standardized collection of routines and policies written in the documentation of WDM. In this model, drivers must provide routines for features such as plug-and-play, power management, etc.

- The Different Parts of a Driver – There's nothing special with the tools and methods used in creating a driver. Usually, programmers write drivers using C or C++. Then they compile it using the linker and compiler from Windows DDK (i.e. Driver Development Kit). Although most programmers use command-line environments in developing drivers, you may create your own driver using other IDEs such as Visual Studio. You just have to make sure that your computer won't use Windows DDK in compiling the software.

  Here are the main components of a Windows driver:

  o Unload() – The system invokes this function whenever the driver unloads and frees network resources.

  o AddDevice() – This function links the driver to a certain device within the network. The device can be physical or digital (e.g. a keyboard, a virtual volume controller, etc.).

o DriverEntry() – This part starts the driver and the information structures it will use. The operating system loads this function automatically once the driver has been loaded.

o Dispatch Routines – This part takes care of IRPs (i.e. Input/Output Request Packets), which is the main information structure used in I/O drivers.

The Rootkits

Now that you are familiar with the architecture and framework of Windows drivers, you're ready to learn more about kernel-mode rootkits. In this part of the book, you'll discover the methods that rootkits employ to access and manipulate the kernel of Windows computers.

What is a Kernel-Mode Rootkit?

Basically, a kernel-mode rootkit is a malicious binary that runs at the highest access level available in the machine's OS and CPU. Similar to a user-mode rootkit, a kernel-mode rootkit needs a binary application. This application can be a DLL or a driver that can be invoked by the OS or loaded straight to the targeted process. After loading the driver, the malware will reach the computer's kernel. Thus, the rootkit will be able to guarantee its survival by altering the functionality of the OS.

Kernel rootkits possess distinct characteristics that make them hard to detect and eliminate. Here are some of these characteristics:

- Stealth – This characteristic helps hackers in gaining access to a computer's kernel. Because most antivirus programs, host intrusion detection/prevention systems, and other types of security products monitor the kernel closely, rootkits must not trigger any alarm or leave footprints.

- Persistence – Hackers who use rootkits have one goal in mind – to establish a persistent access on the system. If these people don't want this kind of access, they won't spend time and effort in creating a kernel-mode rootkit in the first place. Based on this assumption, kernel-mode rootkits are usually well-planned. These rootkits also possess features that allow them to survive system reboots.

- Severity – In general, a kernel-mode rootkit uses advanced technology to destroy the integrity of a computer at the OS-level. This isn't just a problem for maintaining machine stability. Eliminating the malware and restoring the machine to normal can be extremely difficult.

The Problems Encountered by a Kernel-Mode Rootkit

Programmers who create kernel-mode rootkits face the following problems:

- A machine's kernel doesn't have any error-management system. Even simple logic errors can lead to a system crash.

- Because kernel drivers operate close to pieces of hardware, attacks in kernel-mode are prone to portability concerns (e.g. OS builds/versions, architecture (e.g. x64, PAE, non-PAE, etc.), and underlying hardware.

- Drivers that compete for the same system resource/s may cause system-wide issues.

- Kernels are inherently volatile. Thus, rootkit writers need to conduct thorough field testing to ensure that their attacks will succeed.

Aside from the problems listed above (which are sometimes faced by legit programmers), rootkit writers must use creativity and resourcefulness in running their driver and staying anonymous. Basically, hackers must:

- load the driver successfully

- execute the driver

- stay hidden

- ensure the malware's persistence

These problems and goals don't apply in user-mode kernels. That's because the whole "user environment" is designed to sustain computer sessions and prevent system crashes.

Loading the Driver

Before a rigged driver can perform its functions, it should reach the target's kernel first. How can a kernel-mode rootkit accomplish that? This question involves a lot of answers and intriguing possibilities.

Rootkits don't just begin in a computer's kernel. They require a binary or another malware to initiate the loading procedure. Programs that serve this purpose are known as "loaders." A loader can accomplish its task in several ways, depending on where it is located (i.e. inside an installation file or placed directly on the machine's memory) and the access privileges of the profile being used. It may load the rootkit as a legitimate driver, use an undocumented API function, or utilize an exploit.

Since drivers play an important part in any machine, operating systems are designed to allow drivers to load. The computer manages the loading procedure through "services.exe" or SCM (i.e. Service Control Manager). Ordinary programs load drivers by contacting the SCM through an API (e.g. Win32 API). However, only users with admin privileges can load drivers this way. Obviously, rootkits can't use admin privileges all the time. Hackers solve this problem by escalating the privileges of the profile they are using.

Performing Its Functions

Once the kernel driver has been loaded, the kernel-mode rootkit functions according to the rules applied on the machine. It should wait for Input/Output to happen before it can execute its code. This is different from user-mode kernels, which run constantly until the task is done and the loading process ends itself. A kernel driver runs as a calling thread that started the Input/Output event.

Basically, rootkit writers should know how execution parameters work. They should also design their rootkits based on kernel-mode rules.

Interacting with the User-Mode

Usually, a rootkit has a user-mode element that serves as the C&C (i.e. Command and Control) device (also known as the "controller"). That's because something must initiate the driver code, as discussed earlier. If the hacker won't include a user-mode component in the rootkit, the attack won't succeed. User-mode controllers give commands to the malware and check the resulting situation. To prevent detection, many hackers install the controller on a separate machine.

Staying Hidden and Persistent

Rootkits avoid detection by hiding files, processes, and registry keys – things that can trigger the target's defenses. These days, however, stealth has somehow lost its importance. This is a result of the technological advancements in rootkit creation techniques. Modern hackers can inject malicious codes directly onto a computer's memory. They don't have to use any disk or registry to begin their attacks.

A rootkit can secure a permanent hold on its target in different ways. For instance, it may install multiple hooks on various services and/or functions inside the computer. It may also alter the registry, forcing the computer to load the malware during startup. Actually, there are certain rootkits that can go to top-level memory areas (e.g. kernel memory) where antivirus programs won't look.

Chapter 8: What Can Malwares Do?

Now that you know how malwares infect, hide, and reproduce, you're ready to learn the functionality of the malwares discussed in this book. This chapter will explain the things malwares can do on your computer or network. Some of these functionalities have been discussed in earlier chapters. However, since these functionalities are the main reason why malware programs exist in the first place, it's just fitting to end this book with a chapter that focuses on the capabilities of these dreaded programs.

Pop-Up Advertisements

Pop-up ads have affected computer users for many years. The principle behind pop-up programs is to encourage the user to click on the pop-up. Once a user clicks on the pop-up advertisement, he/she will be redirected to a predetermined webpage. The owner of the malware receives a payment whenever a victim reaches that page. Every malware user has an identification number, in which the visits from each malware version are computed, usually in cents. Then, the website owner will pay the malware operator.

Back in 2002, most web browsers allowed users to block pop-up windows totally. Opera was one of the browsers to offer this option to its users; its pop-up blocker can block any kind of pop-up – even the ones you want to see. To enable pop-up windows for certain websites, Opera users had to access the Preferences menu and specify the sites where pop-up pages must be allowed. Many users considered this as an excellent tool in protecting themselves against unwanted page redirections. However, because of technological advancements, hackers were able to bypass pop-up blockers.

The Threats

This functionality doesn't pose direct threats against the user/computer. The attacker simply wants the user to click on the pop-up and visit a predetermined website/webpage. Basically, the hacker doesn't intend to steal information, destroy the machine, manipulate files, or establish a zombie network.

How to Identify a Pop-Up Blocker

The image below shows a basic function that you can use to check the presence of a pop-up blocker on a machine/network. Alternatively, you may use this code to test the effectiveness of your browser's pop-up blocker:

```
function DetectBlocker() {
var oWin = window.open ("","detectblocker","width=100,height=100,
top=5000,left=5000");
if (oWin==null || typeof(oWin)=="undefined") {
return true;
} else {
oWin.close();
return false;
}
}
```

How to Bypass Pop-Up Blockers

Dishonest marketers constantly look for ways to bypass pop-up blockers. Some of these people create pop-ads using the Adobe Flash technology. In this approach, the system won't detect any pop-up and the ad will run in the active window.

Here are additional techniques that hackers use to bypass typical pop-up blockers:

- Pop-Ups that are based on Java – Java (i.e. one of the leading programming languages today) allows hackers to embed pop-up ads inside simple animations. Here are two code snippets that you can use to create pop-ups:

```
function launch () {
target="/xyz/xyz"
y=window.open (target, "newwin", "scrollbars=yes,
status=yes,menubar=no,resizable=yes");
y.focus;
}
```

```
Function openPop(u) {
  newWindow=window.open(u, 'popup','height=540,width=790,toolbar=no
  scrollbars=no');
  }
```

- Pop-Ups that are based on ActionScript – Here's an ActionScript code that you can use to generate pop-up ads:

```
Import flash.external.ExternalInterface;
Function myFunc() :Void
var url:String = "http://www.popup.net";
var windowName:String = "mywindow";
var windowOptions:String = "width:800,height:800";
ExternalInterface.call ( "window.open", url, windowName, windowOptions );
```

How to Prevent Pop-Up Ads

These days, almost all browsers have built-in pop-up blockers. Additionally, users may download third-party programs that can filter advertisements.

Blocking Pop-Ups – A lot of websites utilize pop-up windows to show data without affecting the current webpage. For instance, if you need additional guidance in completing an online form, a pop-up window can provide you with extra details without removing the info you have already entered.

Some internet-based program installers employ pop-up windows to provide software. When visiting this kind of website, read all the details prior to clicking the download link. Hackers may use this approach to send malware that look like legitimate programs.

Page Redirection

Web developers use page redirection in their websites for various reasons. In this part of the book, you'll learn how hackers can abuse page redirection.

Similar Domain Names

Sometimes, internet users mistype the URL of the websites they want to visit. For instance, people who want to access the Google website may type the following URLs: goggle.com, ggogle.com, and googlee.com. Legitimate organizations and companies register these misspelled URLs and redirect users to the right website. Additionally, web addresses such as sample.com and sample.net may point to a single website such as sample.org. This approach allows website owners to "reserve" top-level domains.

Transferring a Website to a New URL

Webmasters redirect webpages because of the following reasons:

- They have to alter the domain name linked to the website.

- They want to use a new domain name for the website.

- They want to combine multiple websites.

Hackers, however, use page redirection for malicious purposes. These people use redirection to acquire web traffic illegally. In general, hackers accomplish this trick by purchasing expired domain names. After acquiring a domain, they will redirect its webpages to another website. Thus, people who want to visit the old site will be forwarded to the hacker's webpage.

Collecting Information about the Site Visitors

In general, website servers record some data about visitors – their location and their browsing patterns. Often, these servers don't record how visitors leave the website. This is because web browsers don't have to communicate with the site's server whenever a user clicks on an outgoing link (i.e. a link that leads to a different website). However, hackers can capture this data in various ways.

The first approach involves webpage redirection. Rather than forwarding the user straight to the proper location, the redirection link may point to a page on the original domain. This process records the links that were followed by the forwarded visitors. Hackers may use this approach to identify sites that can be attacked. Alternatively, you may utilize this approach to collect information about a person or organization that visits your site.

From a hacker's point of view, setting a network so that it logs all outgoing traffic is smart. From the perspective of a security analyst, however, this technique is extremely useful in investigating malware attacks.

Boosting Search Results Rankings

In some cases, hackers modify their webpages to attract search engine crawlers. This way, they can boost their overall web traffic by catching people who don't know how to run online searches. Attackers have used redirection techniques to fool online searchers. For example, misleading data entered in a website's keyword or meta content section can trick online users into visiting a site. Once a user accesses the website, the hacker may attack the web browser, trigger a file download, or ask for confidential information. This approach manipulates the result of an online search to attract victims to the website.

Hackers have also used page redirects to steal the ranking of a popular site. Once this is accomplished, the attackers may trick website visitors into providing confidential information.

Manipulating Website Guests

Since page redirection forwards visitors from one webpage to another, hackers can use it to execute phishing attacks. This method takes website guests to pages that contain malicious programs.

The Attacks and Techniques Involved in Page Redirection

Modern hackers utilize various techniques to forward visitors to certain webpages. In this section, you'll learn about the admin features available in computer networks. Then, you'll know how hackers use these features for their malicious intentions.

- The Refresh Meta Tag – Hackers often use the refresh meta tag to redirect website guests. The image below shows a basic tag that administrators use to refresh the data on their site. News sites use this method to make sure that visitors will see fresh content.

```
<meta http-equiv="refresh" content="600">
```

You can use the tag given above to redirect users to a different site. You just have to include the URL of your target page in the tag. The main advantage offered by this technique is that it doesn't generate any pop-up window. That means hackers can forward visitors to dangerous sites easily and stealthily.

- Manual Redirection – This is perhaps the simplest redirection technique currently available. Here, the hacker asks the website guest to click on an outbound link.

    In most cases, malicious websites are interconnected. For instance, piracy websites that focus on cracked programs or bootleg movies will usually link to porn sites. This strategy allows dangerous sites to boost their overall traffic and profitability.

- JavaScript Redirection – The JavaScript language allows hackers to display a different webpage in the user's browser window. Some hackers use this scripting language to implement page redirection on their targeted sites. However, refresh meta tags are superior to JavaScript when it comes to redirecting online traffic. This superiority results from three major reasons:

    o Meta tags offer more stealth than JavaScript codes

    o Some web browsers are not compatible with the JavaScript language

    o Many search engine crawlers don't run codes written in JavaScript.

- Frame Redirection – Hackers may also use HTML frames that contain the landing page. Here's an example:

```
<frameset rows="100%">
  <frame src="http://www.example.com/">
</frameset>
<noframes>
  <body>Please follow <a href="http://www.example.com/">link</a>!</body>
</noframes>
```

In this method, the browser's URL bar displays the address of the frame file, not the address of the targeted page. Security experts refer to this method as "cloaking," since it displays a credible-looking link to the website visitors.

Data Theft

This problem is primarily caused by office workers. These "insiders" use computers, cameras, recorders, and other machines to steal information from their company/organization. Since employees handle confidential or proprietary data as part of their job, they often become tempted to use the said information for personal reasons. Additionally, they may destroy or share the information just before leaving the company.

In some cases, employees launch malicious programs inside the company's network to steal information. This type of attack can happen via internet transmissions or removable storage devices. These days, removable storages have larger capacity and smaller size. That's the reason why employees can easily steal information from their employers.

Click Fraud

This online crime involves PPC (i.e. Pay-Per-Click) advertisements. It occurs when a user, code, or computer application clicks on an ad repeatedly in order to generate revenue. Most of the time, the victim is not interested with the clicked advertisement. This type of fraud is both controversial and illegal: advertising companies and networks have been sued because of fraudulent activities.

PPC Advertising

In this arrangement, the attackers spread links from ad companies to generate income. As the name of this technique implies, the perpetrators earn money each time a person or program clicks on a link.

Identity Theft

Hackers may use malware programs to support criminal activities such as terrorism, espionage, credit fraud, drug trafficking, and illegal immigration. Some people imitate others for non-financial purposes (e.g. to receive recognition because of the victims' achievements).

In terms of malware attacks, identity theft involves the stealing of a person's log-in credentials (i.e. usernames and passwords) for online accounts. Hackers may use the stolen information to portray himself/herself as the victim. Once this is done, the attacker will steal the victim's money, items, or personal data. Lastly, by getting a person's log-in credentials, attackers may spread malicious programs to people who are related to the initial victim/s.

Identity thefts are divided into two main types:

- Financial – This type involves the bank accounts and/or personal data of the victim. The hackers may steal money from the victim's bank or open new lines of credit. Thus, the hackers pretend to be the victim by using the victim's personal information (e.g. name, address, social security number, etc.).

- Criminal – Here, the hacker uses the victim's identity to conduct criminal activities. That means the perpetrator will be able to avoid capture. Instead of going for the real criminal, the law enforcers or IT security team will search for the victim. In many cases, the victims never learn that they've been victimized by this kind of identity theft.

Keylogging

Hackers use keyloggers to steal confidential information from infected computers. These days, hackers don't have to install the malware on each targeted computer. They can simply install the keylogger onto a single machine and use its microphone, infrared port, or wireless capability to collect keystrokes from neighboring devices.

Here are the different types of keyloggers that hackers use:

Local Machine Keyloggers

These keyloggers are designed to function on the computer's OS. According to IT experts, local machine keyloggers can be divided into three subtypes:

- Kernel-Based – Kernel-based keyloggers are difficult to create. Since these programs stay at the computer's kernel, they are practically invisible. Most of the time, kernel-based keyloggers attack the computer's OS and hardware.

- Linux-Based – Sebek, a popular keylogging tool, is the perfect example for this subtype. Basically, Sebek is a program designed to record keyboard inputs.

- Windows-Based – Windows computers have GetMessage and PeekMessage, two APIs that can collect WM_CHAR data (i.e. system messages that result from keyboard inputs).

Remote Access Keyloggers

Hackers need to install these keyloggers locally onto the victim's computer. These programs are called "remote access" because they can transmit information to distant devices. In most cases, these keyloggers use emails and/or ftp (i.e. file transfer protocol) to send the recorded keyboard inputs.

Ads

Certain types of malware flood computers with pop-up ads. These programs show pop-up advertisements regularly. For example, the browser opens a pop-up window every 5 minutes or whenever the user starts a new browsing session. Others show ads whenever the user accesses a certain site. Hackers who use this kind of malware often earn money by working with advertisers. Advertisers, especially the nefarious ones, sometimes utilize "black hat" methods to increase sales and web traffic.

Many victims complain about offensive or annoying ads. This is because ad-based programs use animations or flickering images that can be annoying and disturbing to some users. Some people actually stop using the internet because of unwanted pop-up windows. Pop-up advertisements for porn sites appear every now and then (which can be frustrating, particularly when your wife or girlfriend sees them on your screen).

Some malicious programs can quietly record user-website interactions (e.g. keystrokes, mouse clicks, etc.). In this case, the criminals will gain direct access to anything the victim does while using the internet. Since these programs can store user information, hackers may use them to perform identity theft.

Conclusion

Thank you again for purchasing this book!

I hope this book was able to help you understand malware threats to prevent them from spreading.

The next step is to check your computers for signs of malware and apply the lessons in this book to avoid infections in the future.

Finally, if you enjoyed this book, please take the time to share your thoughts and post a review on Amazon. It'd be greatly appreciated!

Thank you and good luck!